Health Service

Coloring Book

Adult Colouring Books

Aryla Publishing 2020

978-1-912675-69-2

www.arylapublishing.com

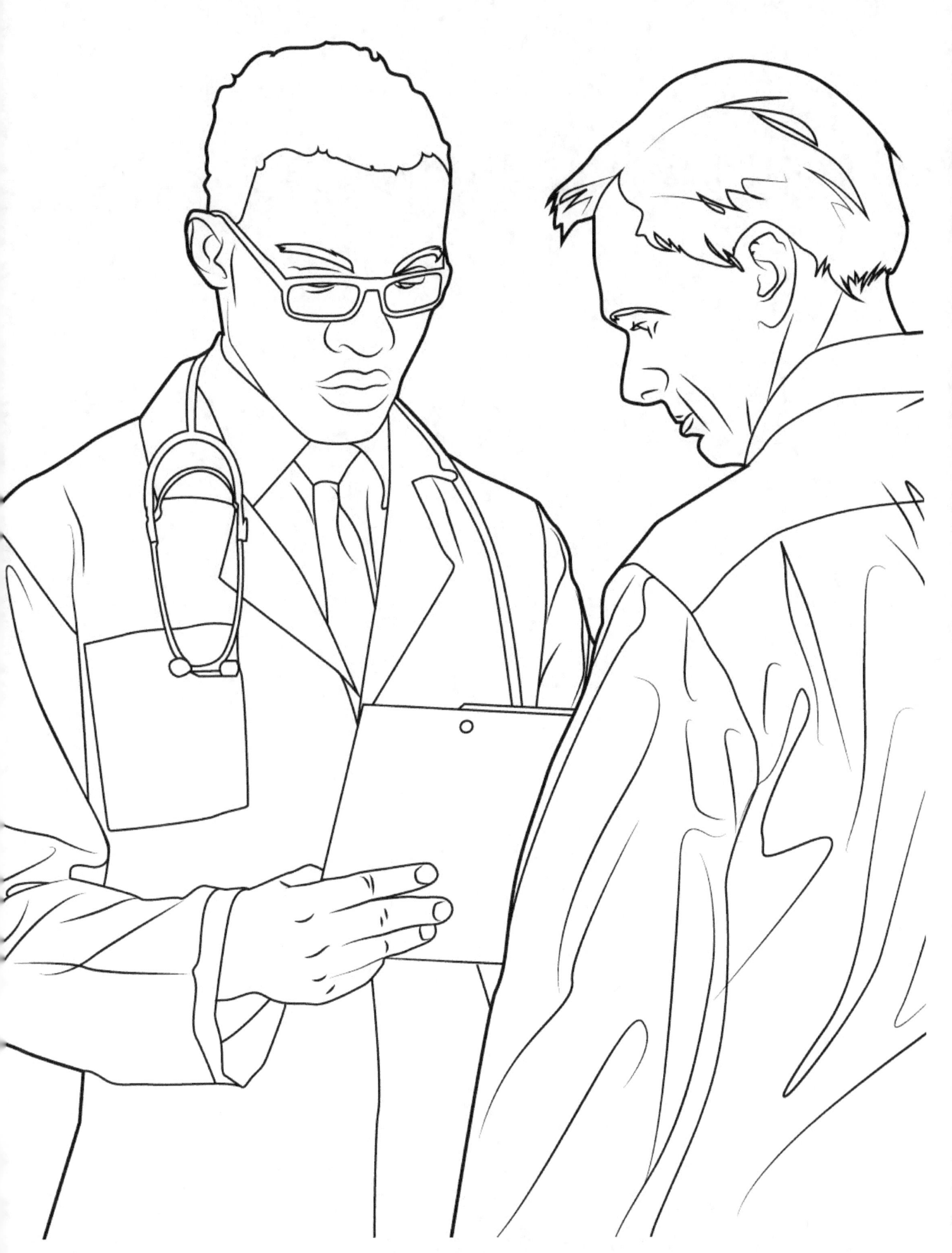

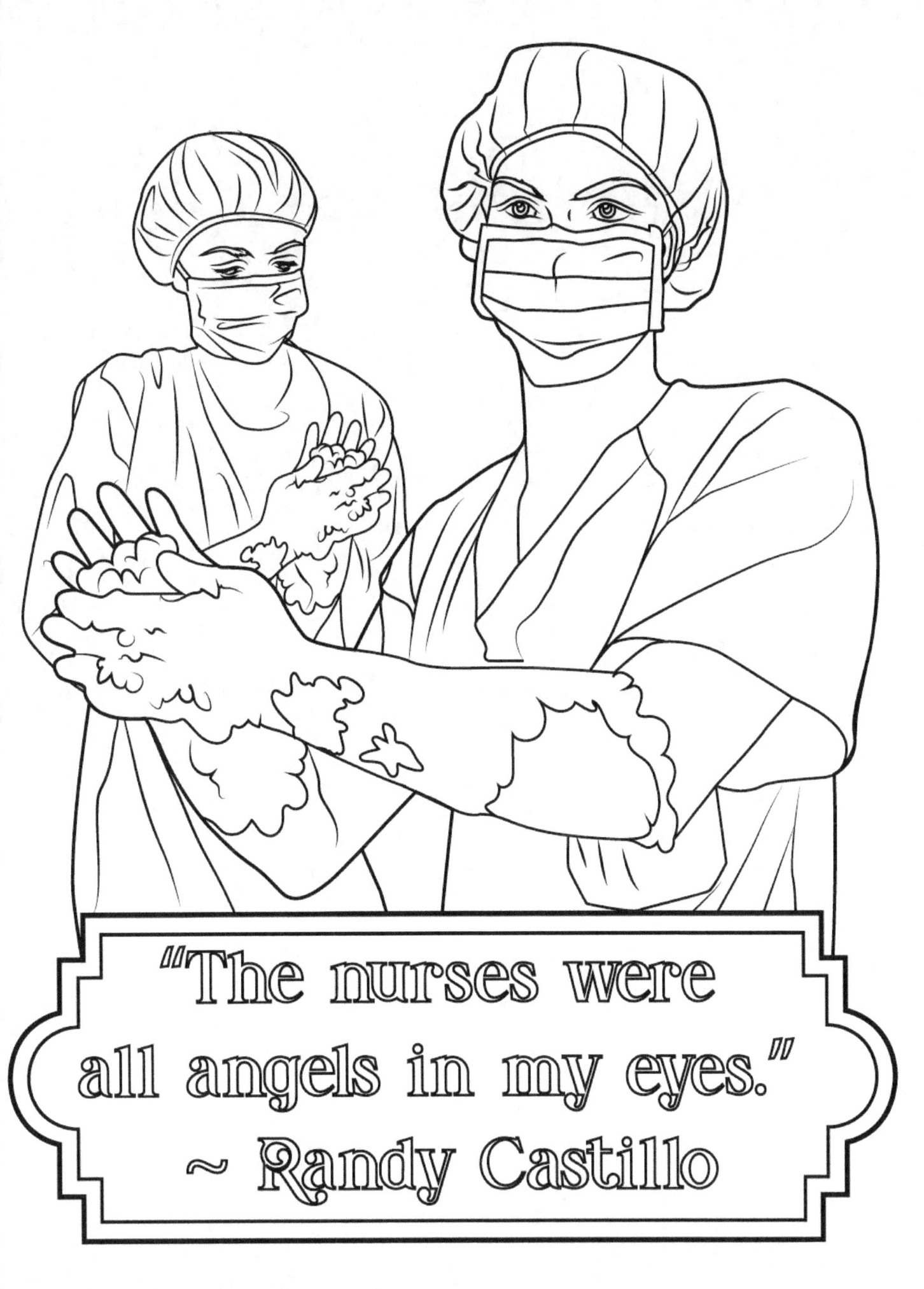

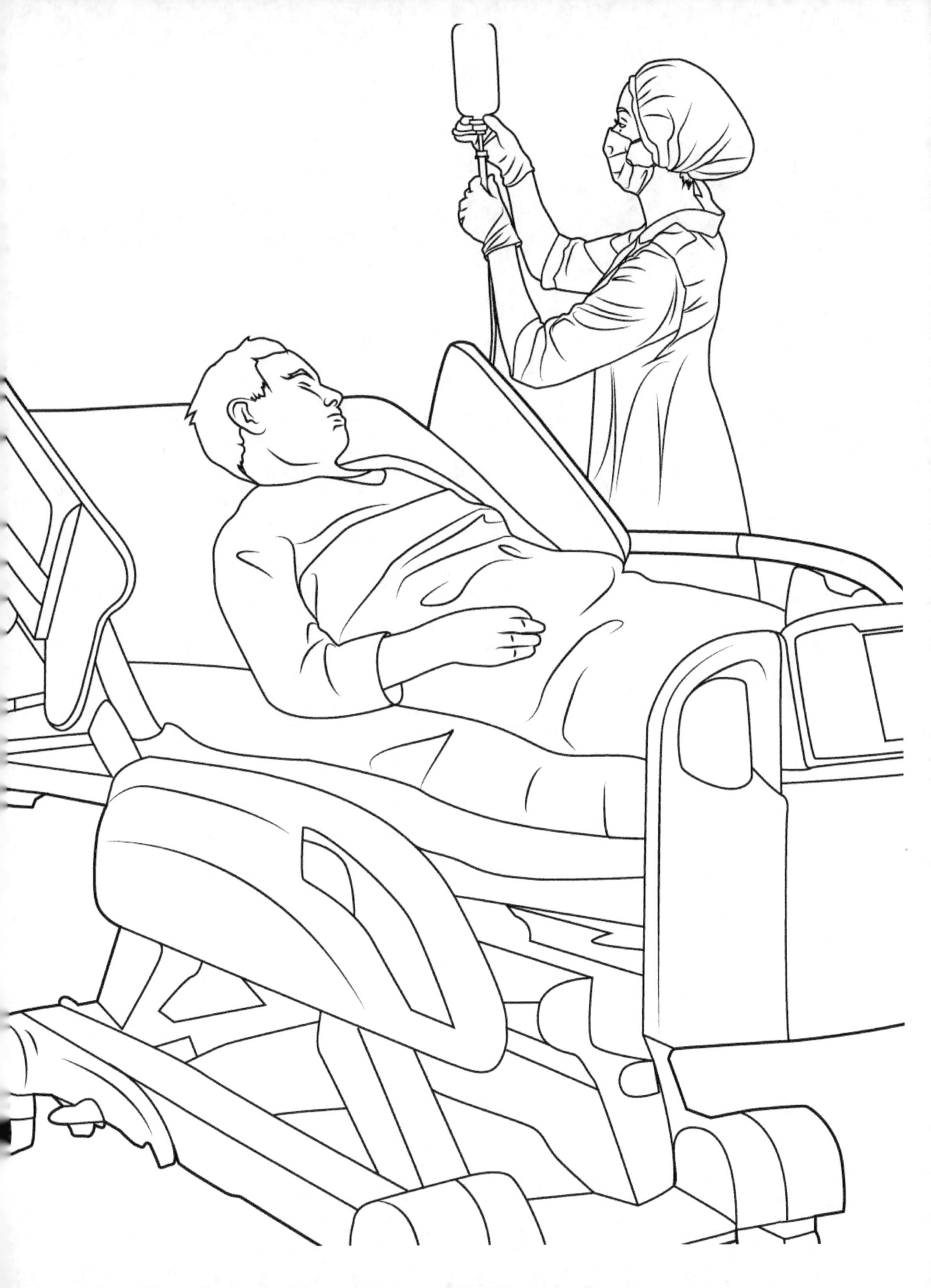

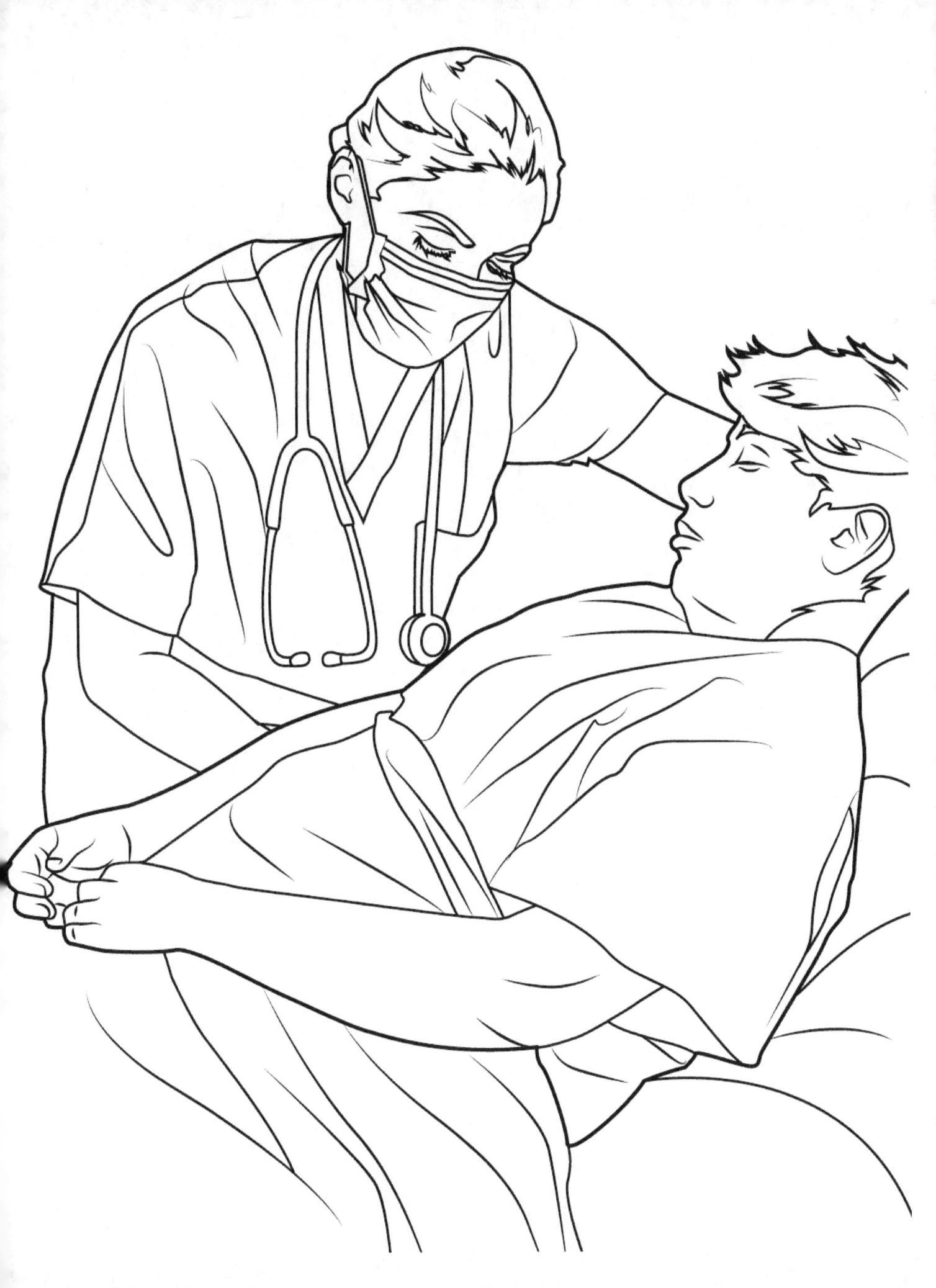

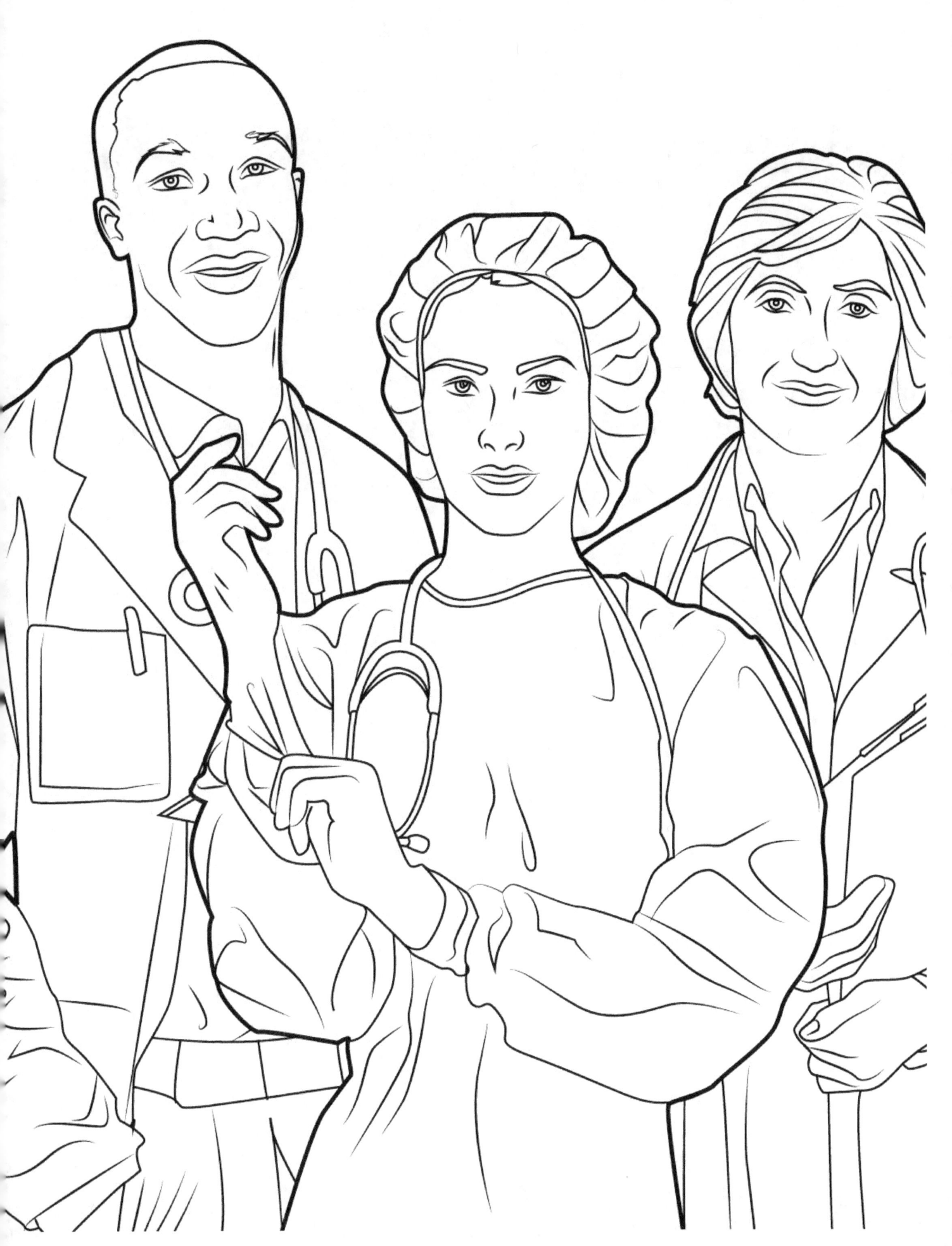

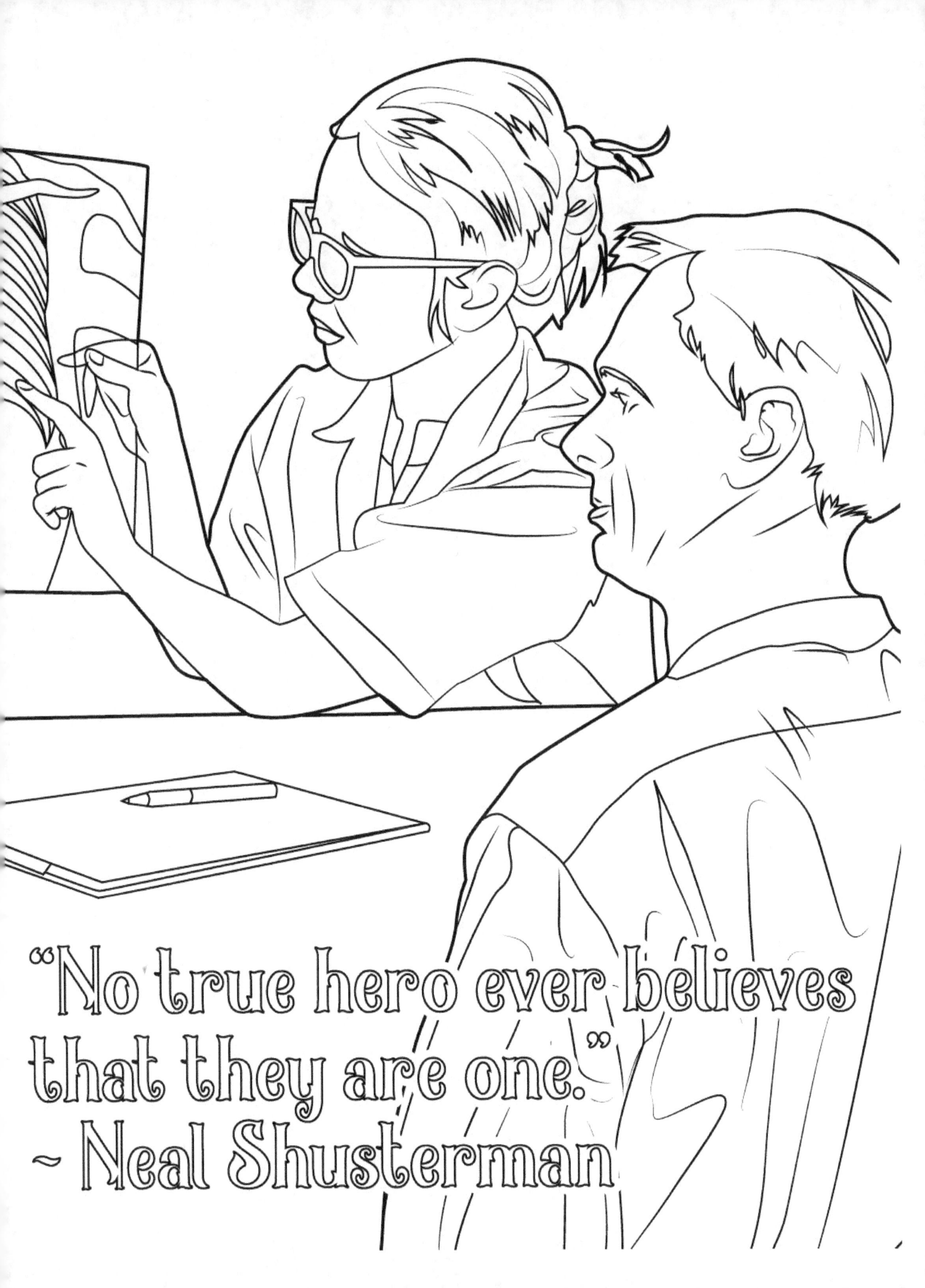

"No true hero ever believes that they are one."
~ Neal Shusterman

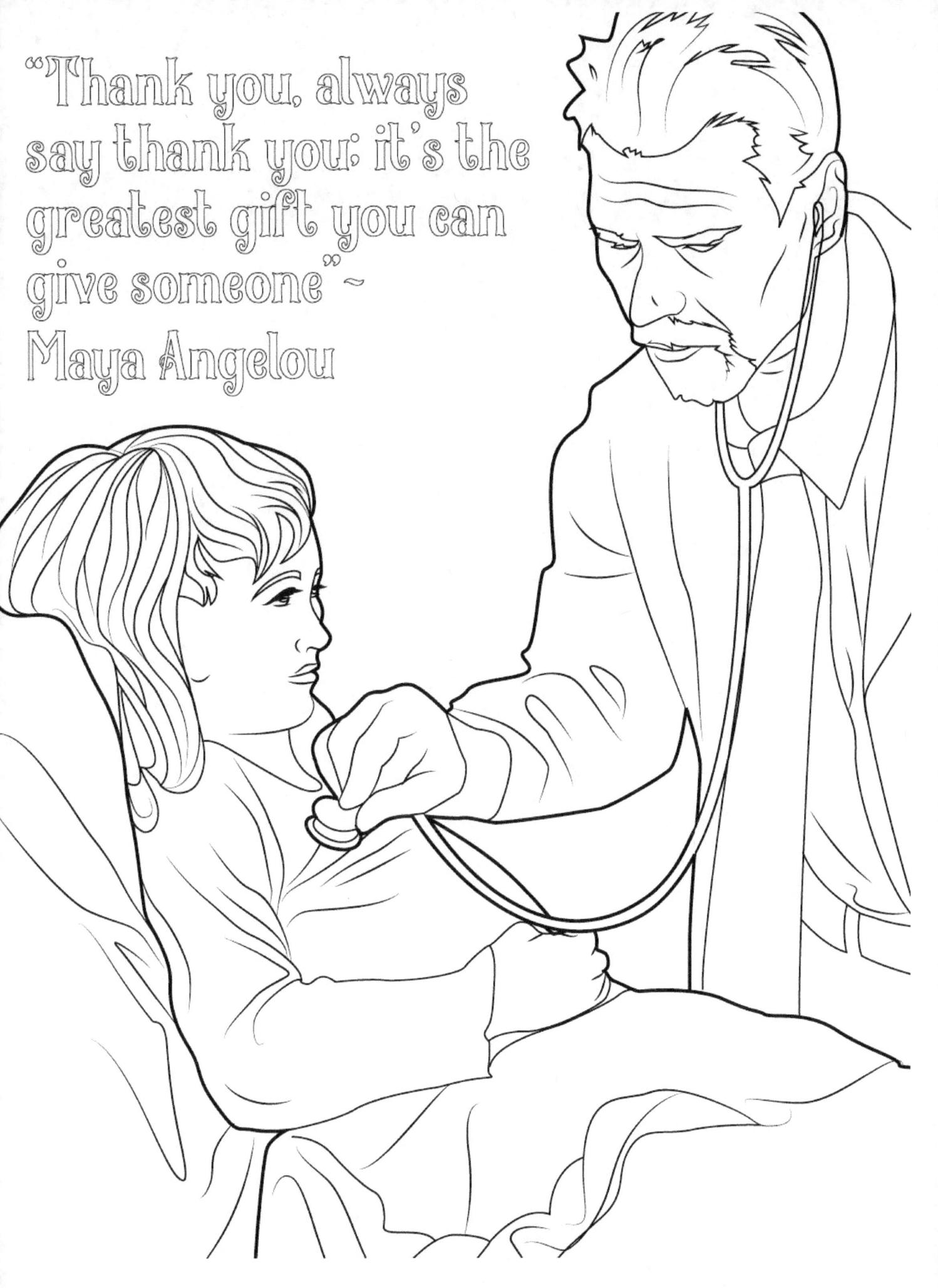

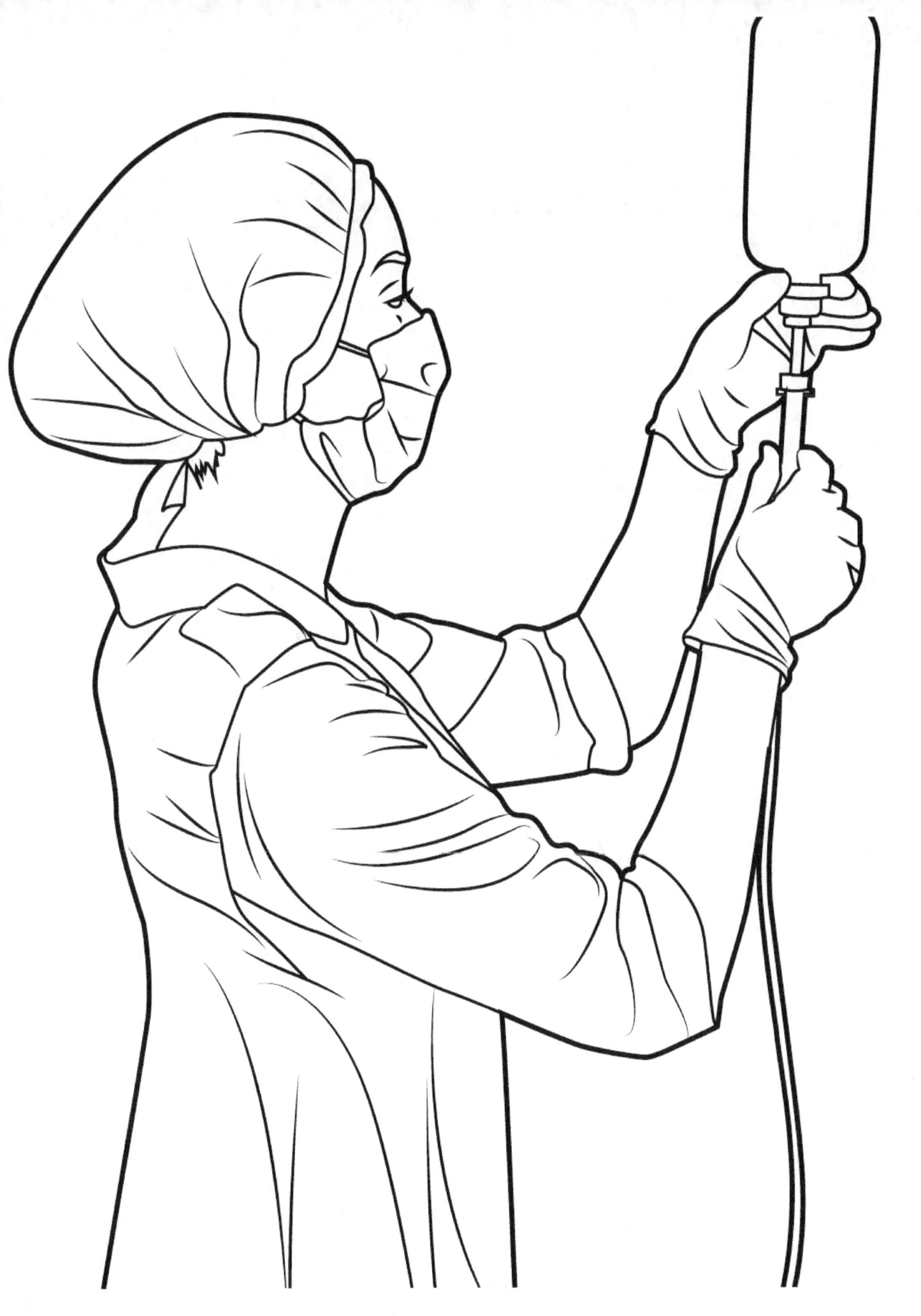

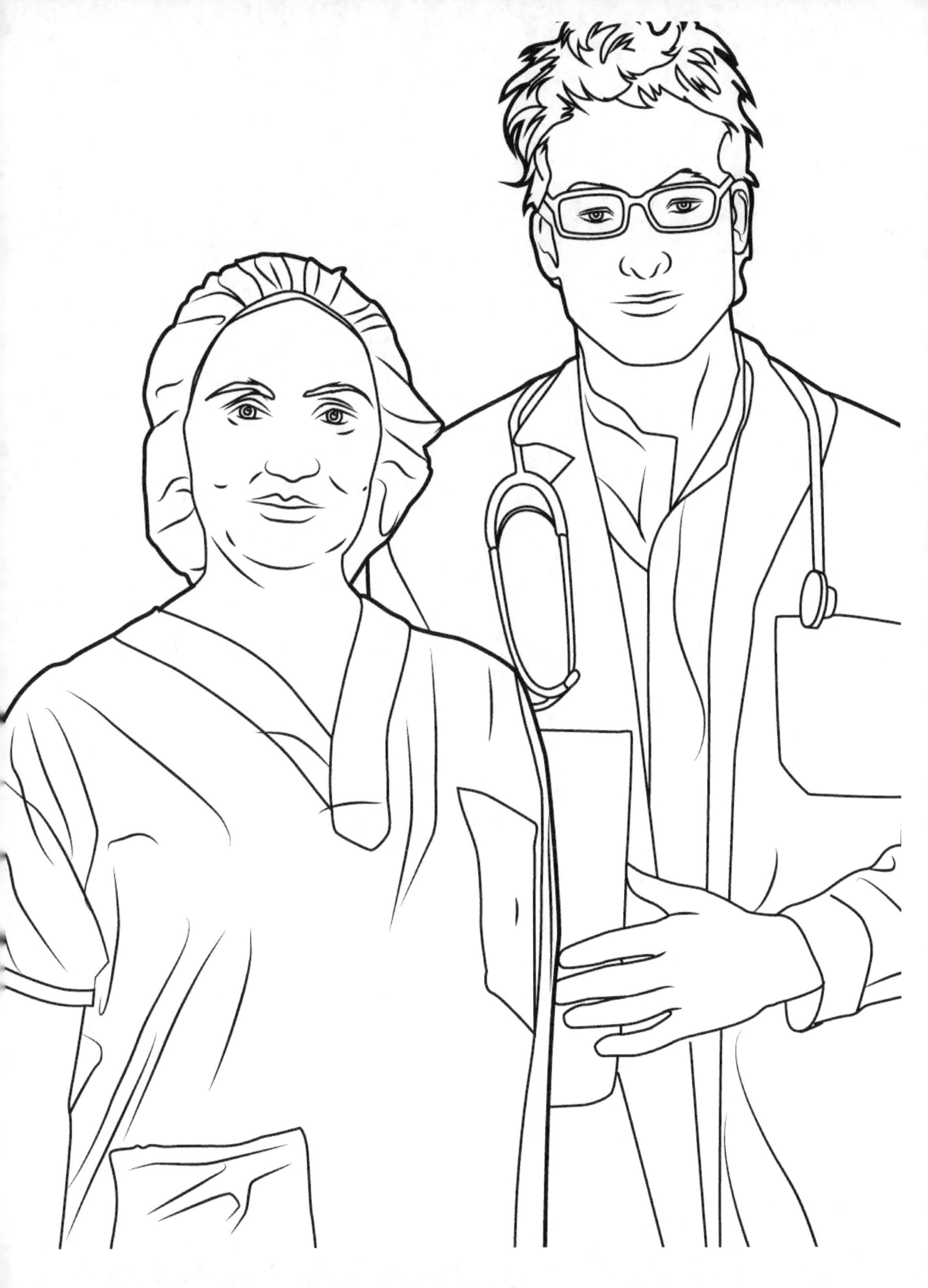

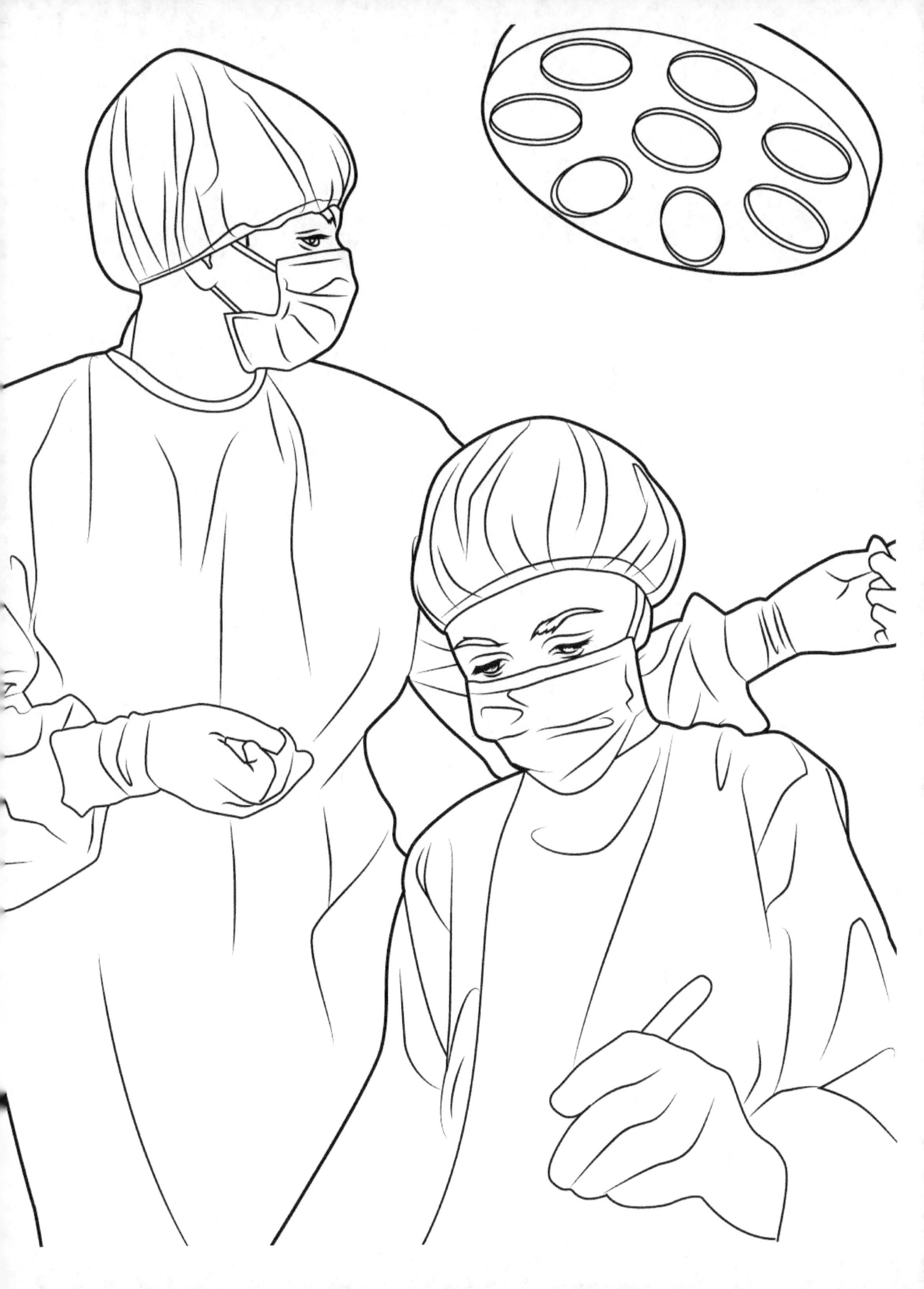

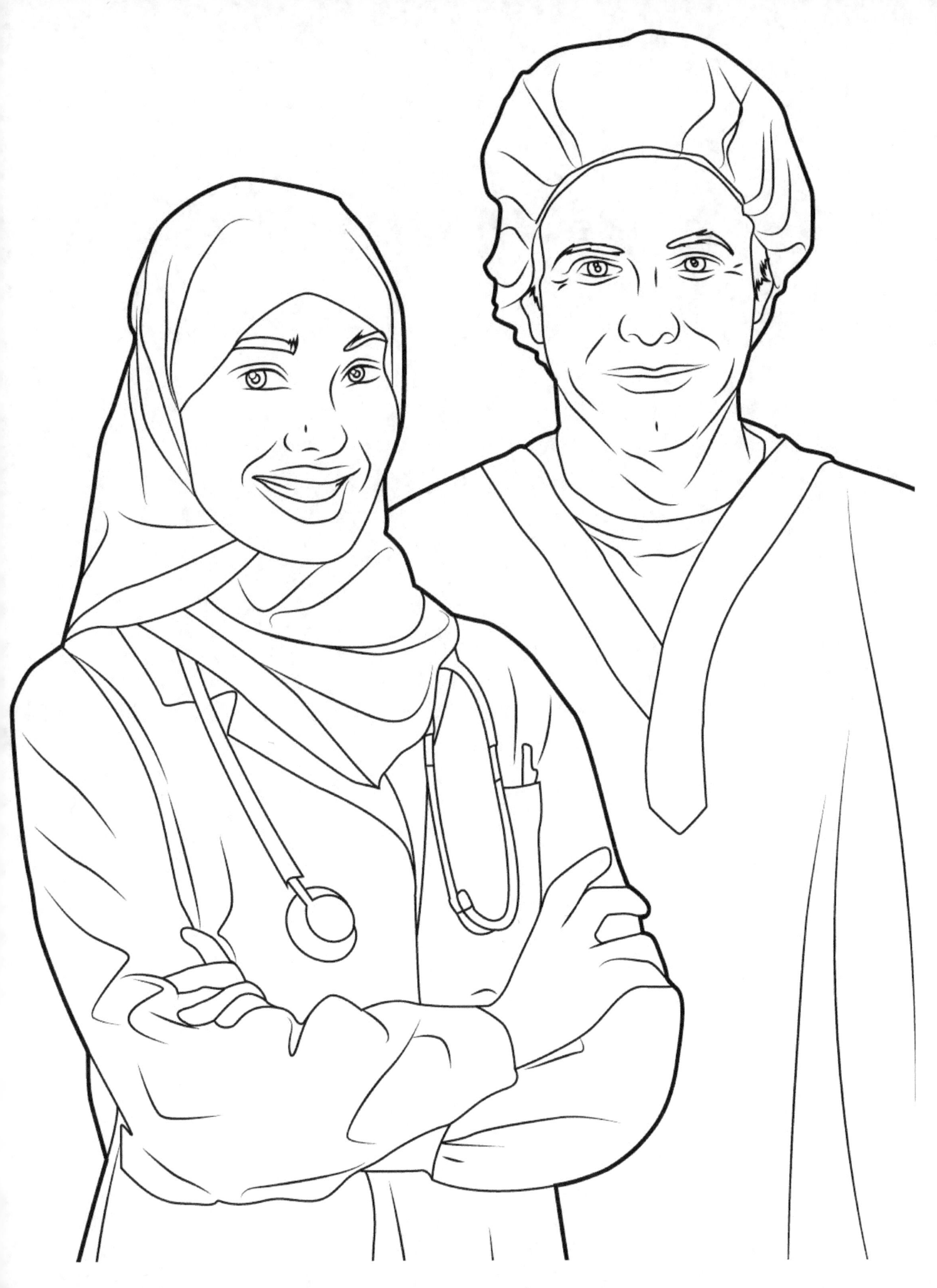

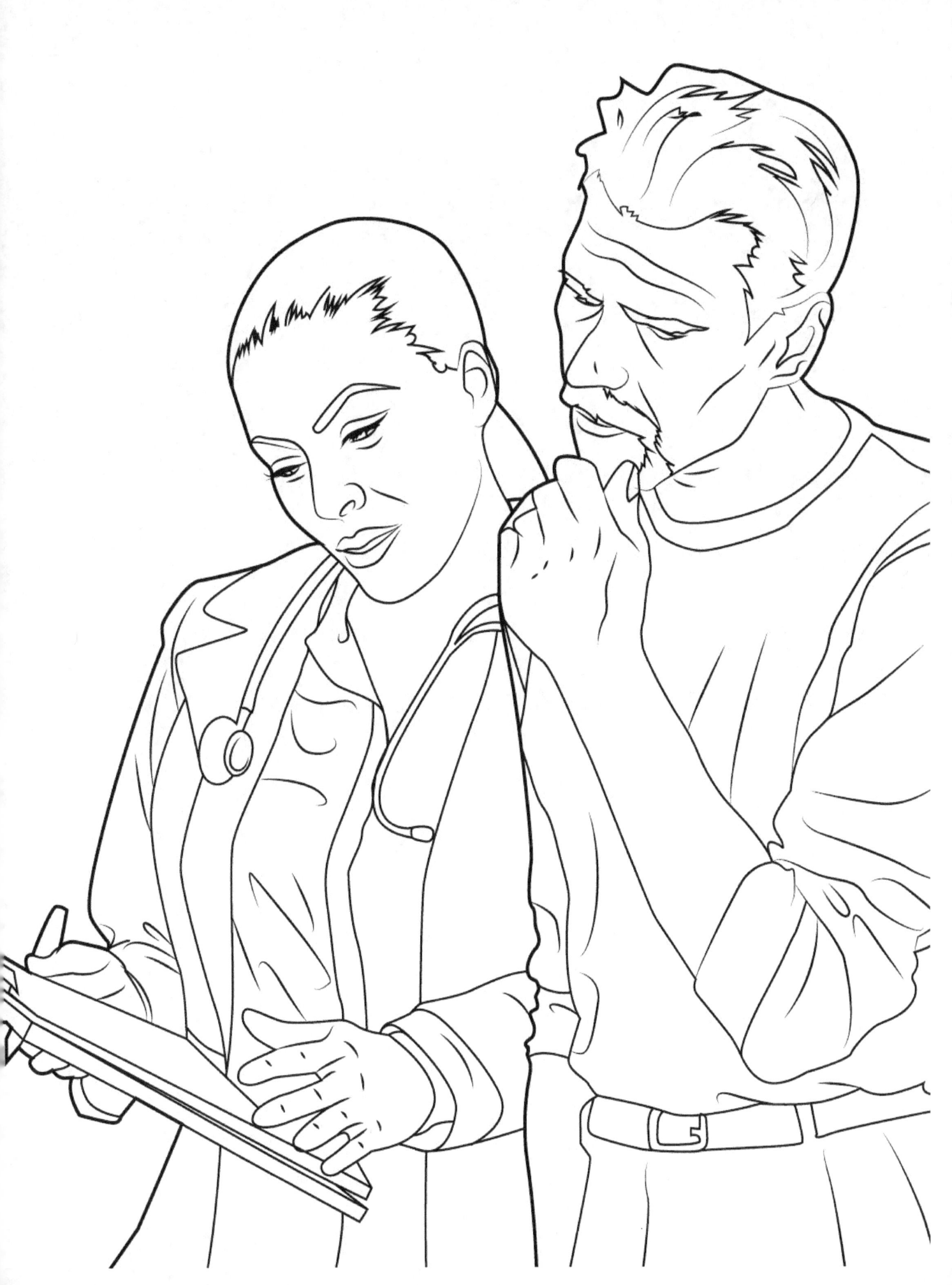

"ANYONE WHO WORKS IN THE NHS HAS SUPERPOWERS"

BENEDICT CUMBERBATCH

"The NHS will last as long as there are folk left with faith to fight for it"

Aneurin Bevan

"A TRUE HERO IS NOT SOMEONE WHO THINKS ABOUT DOING WHAT IS RIGHT, BUT ONE THAT SIMPLY DOES WHAT IS RIGHT WITHOUT THINKING"

~ KEVIN HEATH

"Showing gratitude is one of the simplest yet most powerful things humans can do for each other."

Randy Pausch

"The true hero fights and dies in the name of his destiny, and not in the name of a belief"

Emile M. Cioran

"True heroics, obviously, is not the absence of fear, but having that fear and doing something anyway."

Martin Freeman

"Real heroes are men who fall and fail and are flawed, but win out in the end because they've stayed true to their ideals and beliefs and commitments."

~

Kevin Costner

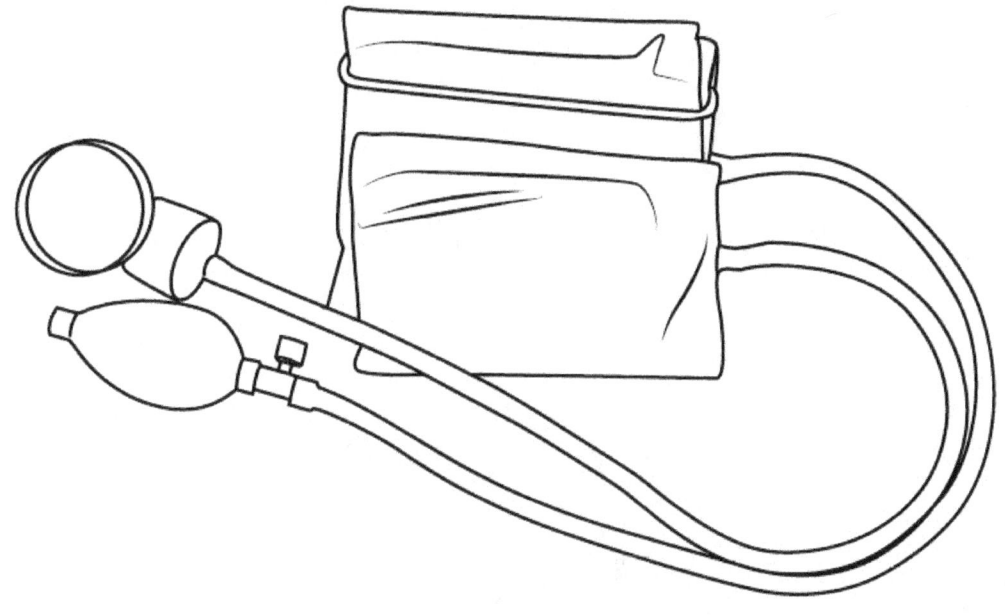

"We must find time to stop and thank the people who make a difference in our lives."

John F. Kennedy

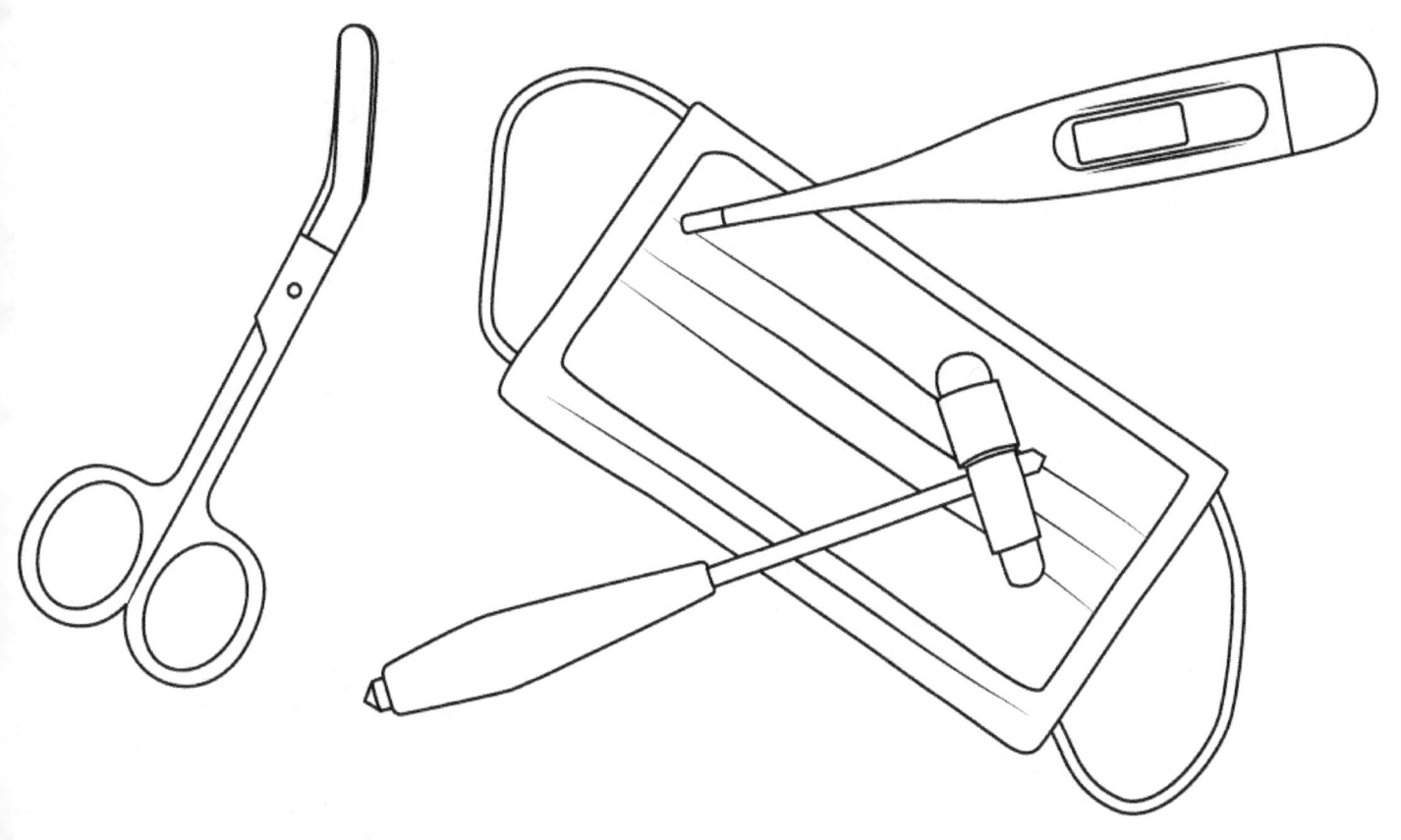

"I learned that courage was not the absence of fear, but the triumph over it."

~

Nelson Mandela

"Life is short,
Life is uncertain,
But we know that
we have today,
And we have
each other."

Eric Greitens

"It is nice to be important, but it's more important to be nice."

John Templeton

"Showing gratitude is one of the simplest yet most powerful things humans can do for each other."

~

Randy Pausch

Other Coloring Books from Aryla Publishing

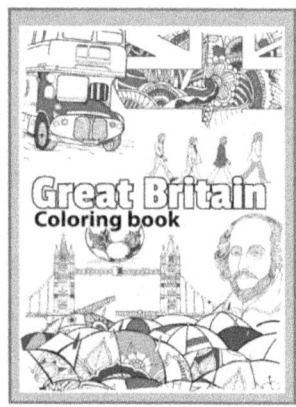
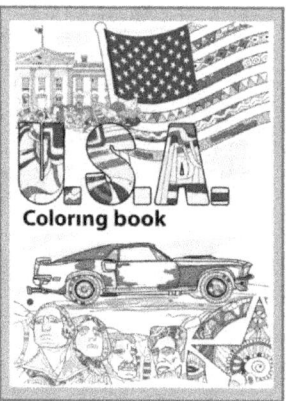
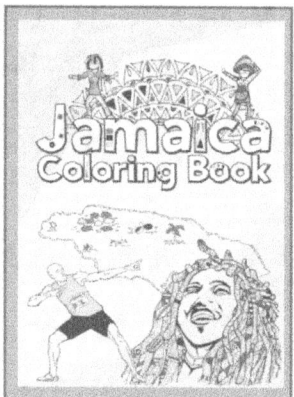
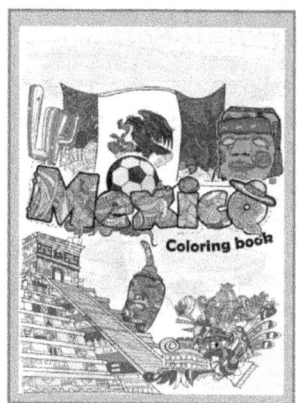

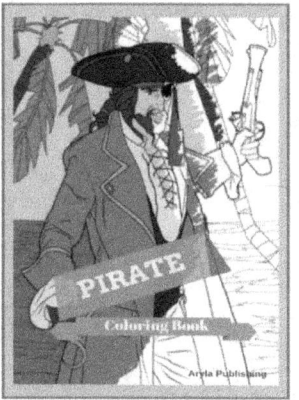
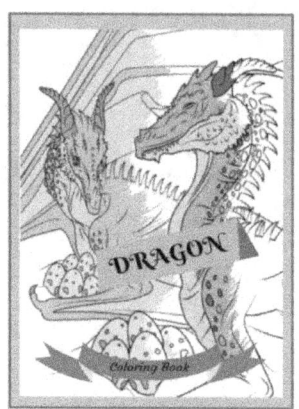
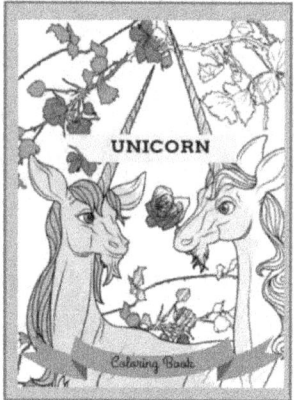
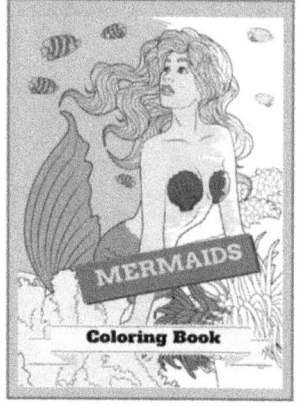

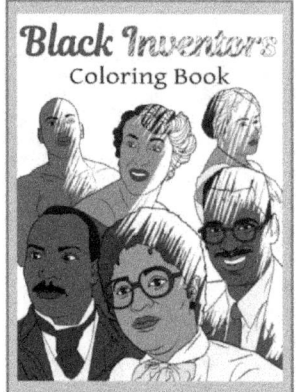
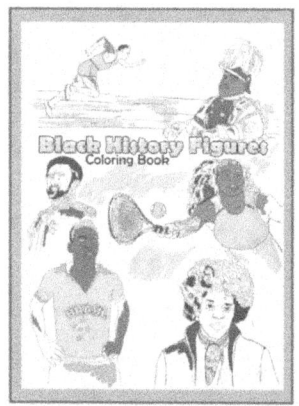
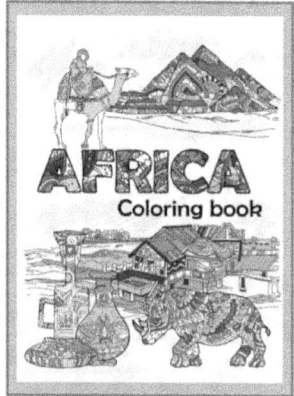
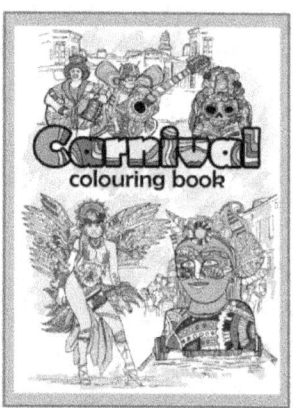

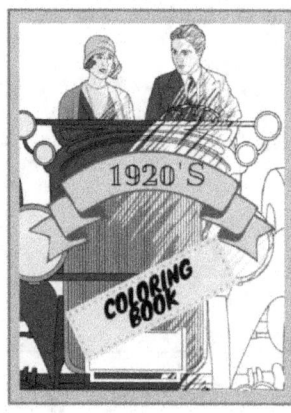
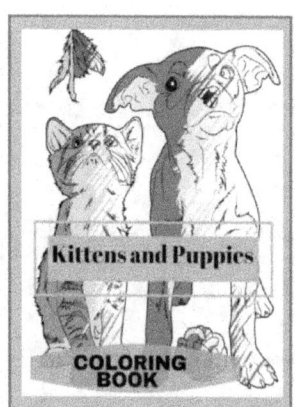
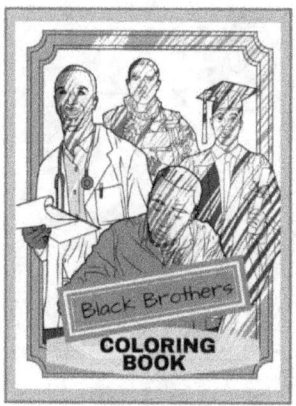
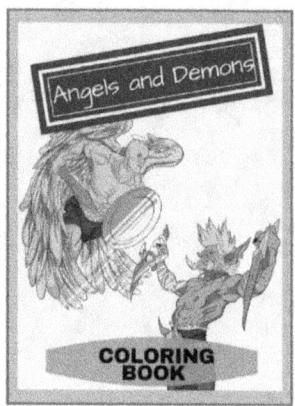

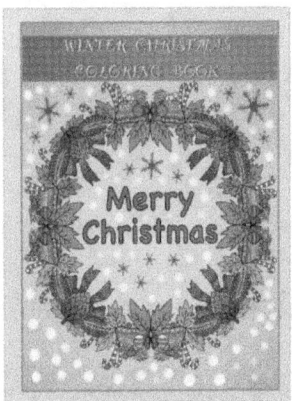

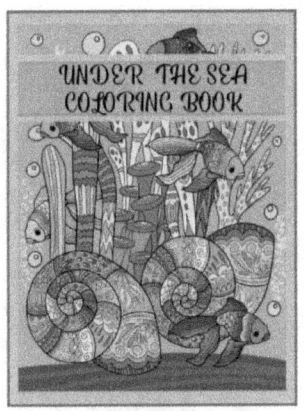

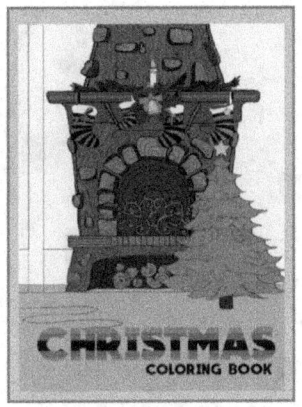

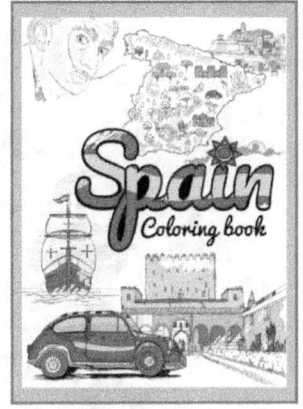

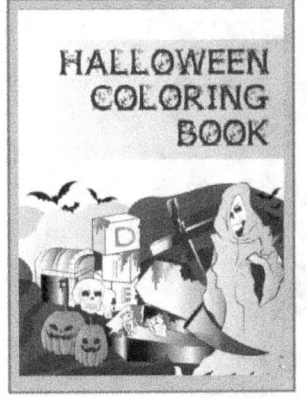

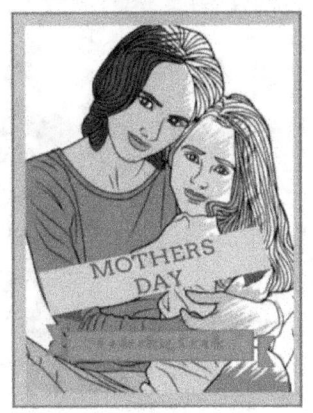

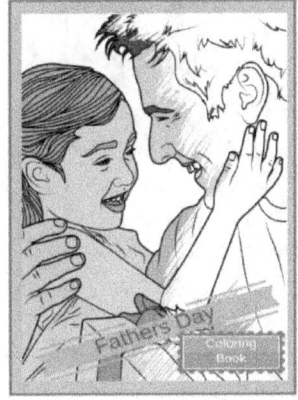

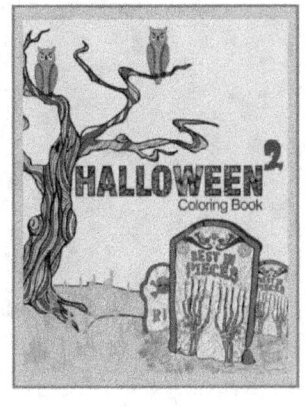

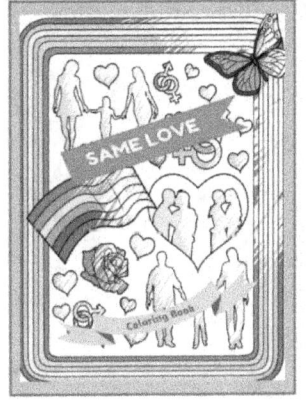

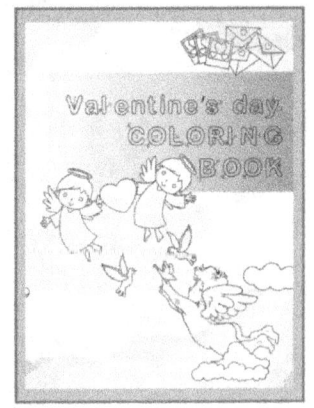

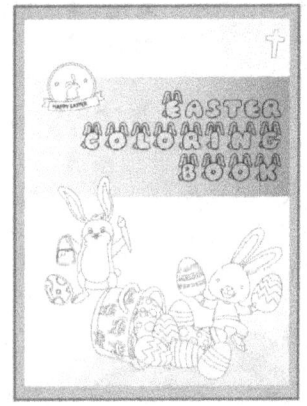

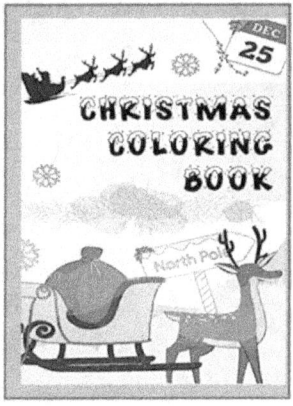

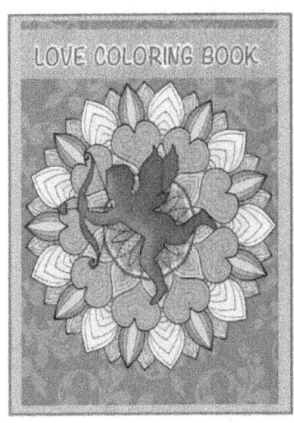

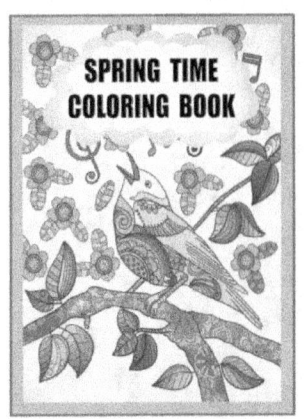

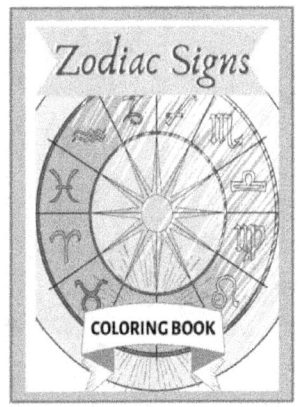

Color In Fun
Kids Books

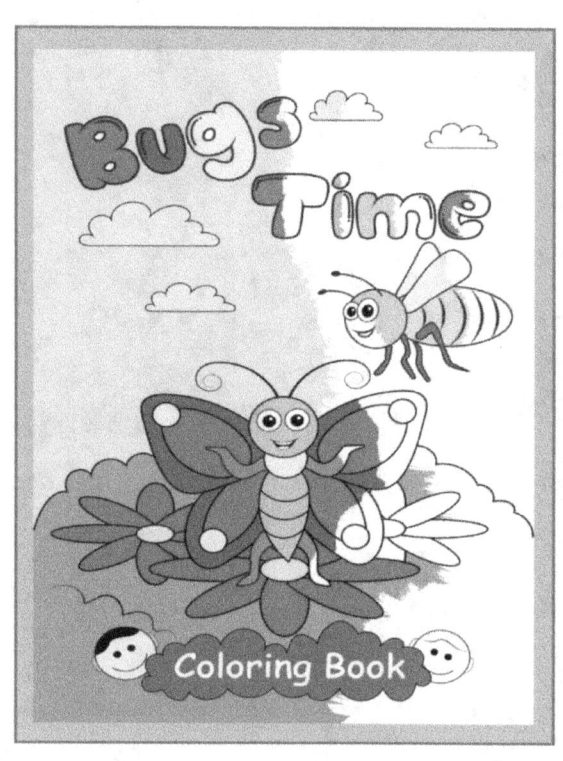

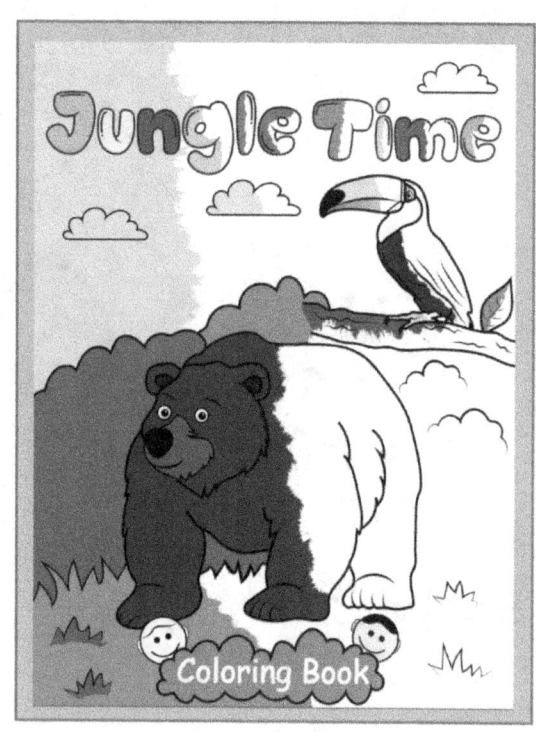

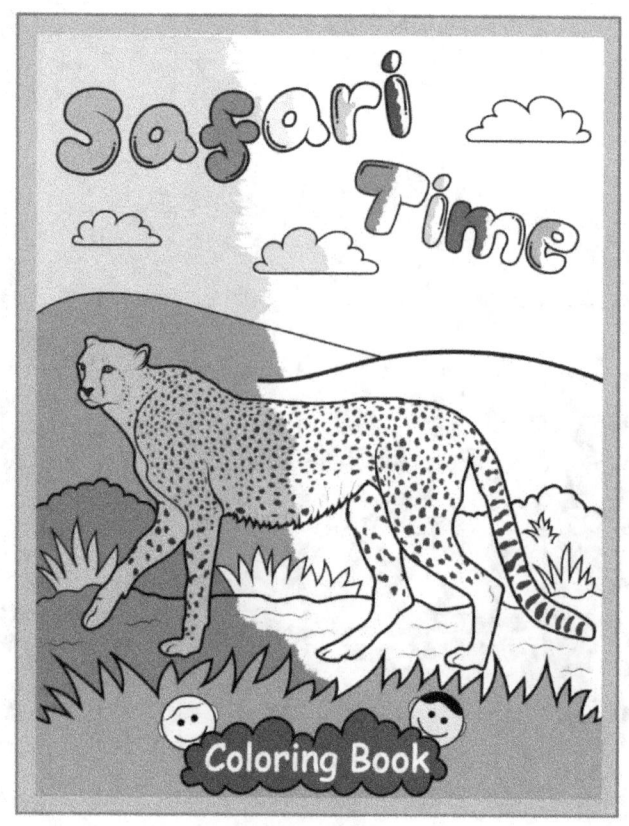

Visit **www.ArylaPublishing.com**
to find out about all new releases.

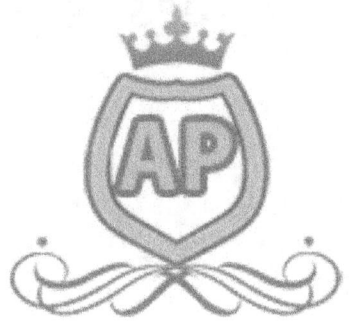

Follow us @arylapublishing on Twitter Instagram & Facebook

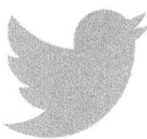  

Search for Aryla Publishing on

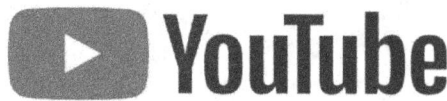 YouTube

Check out our <u>Book Trailers</u>

<u>Subscribe</u> **to keep up to date with new releases!**